Glass Is Really a Liquid

Glass Is Really a Liquid

Bruce Covey

No Tell Books
Reston, VA

Published by No Tell Books, LLC

notellbooks.org

ISBN: 978-0-9826000-1-6

Cover Design: Meghan Punschke

Proofreader: Roxanne Halpine Ward

Contents

Three: Action's Rusty Anchor

Four: Unfulfilled Crossword

Five: Urge

In memory of my father

One: Glass Is Really a Liquid

It's a periwinkle

Tattoo, a periwinkle crop of appliances dusted
Across kitchen fields, where the radio waves won't
Hit, leaving their little static crabs & sanddollars
Far from the AM shore, so you dial your friend
In the scarlet cabinet, sorting the illustrious sweaters
Bearing on them to extract the juice, the fluidity
Of the yarn. Drowsy as an apple, pitched at 45
Degrees & sticky still, sticky with molasses & forks
& watch the tiny ones creeping thru their
Respected wholes. See what the fiber optics can do,
Holding the lot of them with both hands under water
Until they drown & you cook a fine spaghetti supper
With homemade sauce, the kind grandma used to make
After the cod liver oil made you well. & at
The opposite color Batman's silver leaves seem
To point to something beyond the range
Of the human eye, something around the curve
& conceptual, something like a dragon full
Of fire & the desire to keep you teetering
On the edge, the hairline draping lightly across
Each four-letter address, the letter you believe
You sent stamped simply to "Mood," where—
Back to the tattoo—it reflects the very weather
We're having today, dull & canary & vitamin
& swimming because it's there. So, in conclusion,

When grandma bakes the mood pie after silver supper,
She puts on a dragon & listens to sweaters
On the radio, the ones beyond the curve.

Kneeded that

Wipe it down what you just manifested
Two takes because it jitters its nervous
It needs a glass of cranberry it needs two
Solid proteins & belief in rockets & faxes

Wring it by twisting opposites letting
Red drop carry it over & spill it into
Its well wish on the glimmer its rolling
& wooden & three in the earned

Vacuum its shed into the warmest bag
& free everyone to employ it jig it
Square it & tango all the way to the king
Of this particular vertex believer

Sell it in its wrapped excretion flimsy
As outgoing and pooling into questions:
Have you left it with sufficient spectrum?
Do adverbs crawl into soft you speak?

The Most Of

Easy's the first the picnic part of you wrapped in cellophane
Next to the clunking work boots of mean's iconography
To roll out from underneath—thinking the grass & flowers
Have been squished—but a sort of heaven anyway, reclining
Angle, thinking you might be better off walking through
A different door—to choose among the ones with windows & blinds.

So half to the pile & half to the deposit, puzzled into a backpack
& raining, four ever-changing segments under the aura of its
Red hypotenuse: You choose the vehicle by rolling & thanks
For the loan, captured at the edge of its tanager's wing
As if, ok, it's ok for it to rain over everyone else, but me?
What doesn't: sparks, hair, shoelaces, wild ideas

But despite that, why didn't anyone remember dessert?
Whose job was it? & what's the point in meeting
If everyone but you went to lunch together beforehand,
Judge passing a verdict to the jury without
Fact presentations? I'm well loaded with the dazzle of
Shimmying down its cylinder & thanking the time

It took me to ensure you & she were safe
& that, no matter where that, nostalgia for perfect
Attendance, at tube's bidding, polishes the edges
& readies for 30 or so more, mass of it
Suddenly learned via electronic messaging but
Picky because your jammies are already folded so neatly

& in so doing, cancels the baby's challenger

& lives under the guise of balance. So

If you wait for the first branch, I'll grab the other

End Up In

This road, where even the sunlight skidded to a halt
A trudge of friction, or a lack of definition
& 52 open for distribution

Spider webs make this tactile week slippery, to walk
In decline in anticipation of a curve, installations
Of random candy dot the field

& graph habitual, a dollop of vanilla frosting blankets
Your electronic profile—single & overstuffed
With stamps & landscapes, impartial

To extract, sat on a pile of needles in favor of an insight—
Pads wear, circuits migrate & exceed, glance
At the alarm & turn & feed

Nine blankets up to your ears & wrapped in bandages
Underneath, keeping the slices together
Bar to continuous slope, but wish

Simply to let them tile, avalanche of shale
Sliding one at a time under each wheel
Forcing a spin, what direction

Dirt: One that Wiggles a Little Bit Better

Trying to explain the cast of it
Quarter protracted into, say, a wheat field,
In which everything that burrows & everything that quakes
Registers. Part help. Split edges. To the west
Is the virtual cliff one might climb should scaling
Be one's wish. & as luck would have it,
Tipping off the obtuse, this smooth granite
Begets an avalanche. Acute: A stream
Of intent in the form of numerals, eight
Just to point out a single example. One
Burrows one's fingers toward the bitter
Filaments, blanched into translucency
But intentionally porous for ease of absorption.
To push pebble away in favor of vegetable;
Mammal in favor of bird; reptile in favor
Of instinct, a sheet of mica like a tv screen
Projecting into this & that, have & not,
Plus & negative & south & east. With one
Hemisphere in each cup, one pours off
The tide displaced to silver rain

Glass Is Really a Liquid

The one in which a body falls from the top of the fire escape
& something—can you see it?—interrupts

To slow-mo, freeze frame, or TiVo it, a trump card,
The very one you'd extracted from the deck to cast aspersions
On the soothsayer

The one with a goldfish in a bowl, later to be shattered
By descending ice, the day all of the animals
Decided to trudge toward the peninsula

Arms wind-milling only to make the top heavier

The sacred house, the word-down house, the one
With an oak sprouting through its navel & plaster cracking
Floors with pocks and eruptions

But enough square footage to capture all of the titles,
Hexagonal, dodecahedronal, parallelogrammatical,
Arch-nemesis of filtered cigarettes

& snuffed anyway by the wind or rather
Air pushing upwards, if only
There were enough balloons to carry
The thousands protruding, one for each follicle

Or one less? Franklin, Roosevelt, dean of design
& shotglass friendly for recruitment purposes only

Three Ring

It's all the same whether you or me's
The one who lifts it. Ten pounds
Of feathers or ten pounds of dimes—
The one who weighs the more
Will ring a bell of jelly beans.
Yup, a circus theme: The five ways
The stilt man walks, his balance the key
& answer to over 500 questions.
Or the wolf that claims to be
A bearded woman. Fear of being
Torn, howling at the camera's
Flash & brighter than the moon.
Or, shutter speed slow, a record-
Setting lifter, five small & full of aim,
Cigarette-smoking paper bag:
Redeem your tickets here! Skeeball
Or no, the capital of Tennessee's
Root beer is the national bird,
The state bush, the first one to appear
On the 41-cent postage stamp.

Afterpolicy

Numerator's an angel, free to flit about associating
With whomever she wishes, a bucket a cantaloupe
Mars & timber. As luck would have it, Small Equilateral
Wishes the way, pointing, no thank you, to escape.
The roll call will place me at the scene of the crime—
See? She's carving her own ham, her wedding day,
Lacy white & unaccustomed to building her own;
Instead, finding it quite by accident tucked
Between tripping vowels—catching, for instance,
A foot on U's serif. Or, knocked into a flat—
Emergency's wildflowers hissing at the electrical
Current or spit like bacon onto utensil's bearer
Or talk with the guy with the armband
Lurking in the background—surely he's the one
Whose budget is at stake. Clearing, cranked
To sequin's middle or limit—whose pants
Fall without a circle, shut up. For a second—
The edge of the raft doesn't lift you
You collapse into the river, holding
Onto one of the big robes & testing a toe
Gently for moonlight or cashews—a time to
Start the meeting & make concessions

A Beautiful Visit, A Beautiful Injection

The strongest ones are the careful ones—
You need to make them work first.
Lightning in its slippery conduit would strike
If only one of the presidents would pay.
I feel like a glass of lemonade.
How did they come across you?
The yellow pages? In any case,
It's a triumph. Now you need a blanket
& some clever tools to mine this lode!
I thought the return on staying would be
A very special treatment. Now everyone in
The room needs jeans because the lasts
Are ripped near what's embroidered—
Put it on the blackboard, see who comes

Box Springs & Mattress

Climate's climax—carrying a brand new door,
Roto-lock & all. The kitchen's been disinfected
From the lack of one, thinking all the little
Animals might congregate after.

Its pillowcase fabric viscous enough
To repel anything from water to particles.
We elect the refrigerator to adjudicate
Future friction—one's fiction is

Another's freefall folly. A clever
Arrangement of zots, red & black
Defining the central melody,
A couple of tank engines to haul away

Debris, five hundred & fifty tones
Demystified, seven Oscar nominations.
My piano is your piano, my hammer,
Your strings tide-tuned, four fingers deep

& ready to hear the nautilus's final echo.
To be frank, I love your vagina.
It's 2:00 am, you're tired & am I,
The phone rings, it's you, or you

Roll over & it's me—I launch
A paper airplane that lands on your pillow.
You unfold it and read I'm
Behind you's what's missing.

Wish

Tune yr sandwich to the key of C
Make biscuits in kitchen B

Miss Scarlet with her lead pipe
Waits behind the cupboard door

Clubs one from the other limp
Only to begin again innocent

& nothing to do but gather into
Legion gather into constellation

Coming along then a spider its web
Holds the walls together holds the floor

Up gathers toward a central point
Mean & distribution derivation

To insert a thumb & see what sticks
Past the earth's crust cirrus

And acidic enough to spoon fork but
Chew & eat & swallow digesting the fact

That nine wonders hope the clouds have
Answers hope the clouds have

Good for you

I've got lazy console, one the fire wrote over
& scratched only, its arcane temperaments

& stalks, its juicy cosine & cinnamon perimeter
Cracking yet ready to operate, flip no that one

Because even in this recess stalagmite or divot
Might catch your toe & make it, its

So gather & stuff them on this little cart
& wheel it over to the shrinkwrap station

Incense its little alert to tag an implicate order
Bombed-out justice & signal its precipitation

Wagons of it overflow green just because &
Altered to reflect the most important new research

Where cabbage amidst its heart & diamond
& the one who's hungry enough to inflate

Zero-Sum Game

Pumice & basalt are examples of fragmental ejecta.
A nomenclature merely corresponds to more or less
Arbitrarily selected points along
A continuously graduated series.

Inspired by bees, the bony mirror remains wrapped.
The mulberry tree enjoys its "seeing bag"—a red, silk square.
Slow aluminum fires are one of the hazards
Of this thermomechanical pulping process.

A singular hole squeezed & pulled apart,
Bent to form the spring, cooled & reheated
To make it flexible. Other forms are pink
& galvanized, asymmetrical, invisible to the operator.

Proofs & Manners

To unfold the napkin to discover a pistol in the bathroom
To unfold the paper & revisit the stock exchanges,
Mine up & down & forward & backward

To unfold a grey triangle into circles of primaries
It's yellow to the degree where you stand, multivectored
Oaks cutting into those gestures with which
You've charged all of this atmosphere's nickel

To inquire about a derivative, one you can sip
Through a flexi-straw, & the strawberry's flesh & seeds
Ordained with double dactyls & the backs of ten

With an ornament here, and an ornament there
This one glass and this one brass, to unfold
Its spirit out of its tide, the currents buffeting
Starfish up against it, cloying an unexpected divot

To unfold this tent: Tab A from Tab B, center
Pole, drive spikes with a granite stone to seal the exegesis

Or will only its flap keep you dry? It's pouring
After all, the flan is soaking even though you promised
Me it wouldn't rain, and trusting you, I left

All of my loved ones out on that bench

Notes to Section One

1.1 If targeting a non-English platform, titanium scalability enables native communication.

1.2 The next draft will be structured as a superset of the declarative Tiny language.

1.3 Just as if you were really there, blue marble winds unencumbered access.

1.4 Subversion fixes binary mirrors and antelopes, spins readings incrementally.

1.5 Dime's two opinions: Perfect condition, not a chip, crack, or anything broken.

1.6 Half-life steam, because some mirrors might require that you do not block.

1.7 Aiming for denial in various aspects of royal cryptography, confidentiality, & integrity.

1.8 Stephen Hawking held it together in a zero-g vomit comet. Black on black—Which is more?

1.9 For use at various singing events like church. Orange you min?

1.10 A blizzard would balance & add new cube recipes.

1.11 Reduced drops in the cow pasture, monsters and threshbuckets.

1.12 Mutagen is a pylon, a parsed trove & its odd theory, pear cheese, speed & thread orbit.

1.13 Or as Brenda says, text minus & bacillus aspirate, while citrate temple cycles.

1.14 Dealing with lactose withdrawal is in the constituents' upper interests.

Two: The Greek Gods as Streaming Data

Ahead of the Curve

Why don't lime & life rhyme?
Why does the end matter more than the beginning?
In the skintight pants, the ass flexes.
With a score of its own, the sheet aligns the chords
Into a healthy something, carrots for the eye
& progressive sleep, the saturation of scratches
Into this neo-realist interpretation
The olive oval & protracted coconut
Because of the track, each single foot
Delineated & parceled & brimming with nightmare,
The kind that predicted all of this & all of that & then
More, the subtle lines of the circus tent leading
To the moon, the absorbed &, apart from the killer
Clean curves of the slide that launches you
Into the air & land, two feet before
Every syntactical permutation (green)

Demeter

Burning grains, their various natures, popular with plain
Features—an outline—the casting of decade to day
August's cult, coupled with a passion on a field three times
Pines that stick atmosphere's shell & draw the thread
Combined into a single petal, flexibility revamped
How many euros a leaf? Stationed along the avenue
Mojito, pink lemonade, cotton candy, sex on the beach
Curl of cinnamon's bark, vanilla leaf, walnuts
Made from different wild animals and furious lot casting
Shaped like a vault, but pulled vertically by a cable
By exploiting innovative glue, this apparent paradox
One that builds its own diamonds, jack of soldering iron
100 stems on the threshing floor, the trigger for a trap
& can of wheat. Sweeping waves of its tender tips in
Farming conditions quite by chance. The reductionist's view
Might wholly embrace its circles at the expense of
Spheres. Date oasis in Tunisia, originated by the typo
In her eye white, palatino, brushed off & discarded
Up the sleeve, apples' burden of the resulting sudden, or
One photograph per day, themselves lacking continuity

Io

Eating out overtakes seismic apples at home
Glanced feather possibly, the right angle of an upper lip
& generate an electrical field line on an active surface
Sour, divided into two bowls, gathered based on viscosity
The ground-based, infra-red coat hanger. Resonates & wobbles
Half her triangle, matched up and down the aisle, torn:
They have 7 kids? A doughnut-shaped torus glows
Implying an empathetic verb, stunning in fleet, modifiable
Tree, garbage-collected language, faster than pearl or ruby
Or titanium. Where's respirator's soup, the cling of
Support actors rewinding the lowest analogue at the door
Its midwife fortunetelling catalogues of minute gestures
Alongside the robust, optimum theft, routed high-speed
Stitches?—length of its pleat & comb of its tulle
Triple play's evolution, your next car and personal trainer
Whisked into the stadium's porcelain bowl, eggs
In the midst of their prism transitions, invisible nets
Catch uncountable perch. Her audience's final caliber
& each with a full bar. Make drink, cat's cradle
Rock paper scissor. Doubled outcome, each of the gold pair
Magic mice and fates, plateworm's encrypted Trojan
Hidden in the belly, but jumping out, scimitars drawn
With sandbox static, various implementations of a useful
Stream—& dittoed before the source runs dry

Clytemnestra

When the signal's given, her torrid affair
In white, the colorlessness beneath the maze
On mountains the next would light & so on
The rise of the bubbles to the rim of the flute
So vehemently electric, stone proceeding
In strings popping, notes carried off the margins
& easy challenges for chalk, animation, a singer
Reckless at the tips of the rope, the fiberoptics
Helped elect #61 when suitable to text, author
& wish that type might be more than a dance
On tiles, coasters, cups, & mugs—Play with me
Or its picture, lit from arrears & glittering fragility
A 14-inch minotaur stuffed, magical, stadium
90-something to vibrate, a muddled machine
On the floor placing pieces of red all around
& animating theatrical apparel, the location of
Our adding machine's dollhouse evening, 2 spiders'
Interlocking messages, engraving audible salt:
A nymph defending herself against elegy

Metis (Possessive)

A fine element mesh produces fill-reducing orderings for sparse
Nation: Dedicated solely to installations, even in the snow.
The irony is that water once surrounded this clump of reeds, still blue
& exercise. There's a catch. Plus-two's state pathology
Clustered by trails—that part's ok—to the 34-day trial
& company's even blank. Sexual harassment, butterflies, erasing
To what was still a wild, "Free through the herd, dedicating
The beasts in favor of an exit poll" & / or swamp-in's ticking
A buried blue. Lesson's "O come all ye" upward barrel, top
Wherever's different; source of material that comprises its planet
& for already boxed on, 60 pounds in the hallway, carrots, four isn't?
Aluminum's breezy precious, causal fabric, nine times ten
As stable's strong decline, shape connoting blood or to mix
Prepackaged tastes into the grilling hamburger, smoke to design
A group of wagons to expose themselves, apprentice & cabinet
& fine with the pixels—grains of sand—to sift into a school
State imaging system's essential oils, a consort puzzle exchange
When, fighter pilot, touch's lifted & procured on slings home
For harvesters, fish & man, or howl's not a magazine or a cup
Although I'd be happy to occupy either as this week's finite chair

Hermes

Surprise! Discover discover discover classic hand-folded
Vermillion triangles, segments digesting their sparkles &
Two white ribbons, later represented by serpents in a figure 8
Knot's packed message, aimed to reveal the truth about
Types of racing, boxing, steel, and backwards in the sky
A millisecond's pull, but on all of the points at once, mirror
Or a daisy spin structure, bound states held together by lyre
& a new track record! 14 speeds, quadruple levitating cams
#04-1170 Kansas versus Marsh argued December decided
Overhead, but with underwater's woozy enunciations
Aimed at professionals, parents falling exception
To the legislation that mandates transparent etiquette & ambiance
Now redirected to grooming Europe's deep-ocean margin
Soprano's tenure, the cream of the financial statement, notes
Who fortified the alarm: A tripod & a cauldron & plenty
Of bright—What the train tracks down, beaming much
Promiscuous apparel, stringing sinews across the wearer
Could bounce a quarter off this calculated epidermis, or
1.3 autohell solaris; 0.7 thank you for your kind understanding

Duotone

Conceptually better positioned than many of the houses in
       Southern Pennsylvania
& overlooking a pastoral persimmon lot
An initiative to address the sudden deforestation of the Congo
       Basin Zone
Where various marketing devices render the ditto useless
Is coupled with seven alert springs, oscillators arranged in a line
& accounted according to height and date of capture
Type "kitchen appliances" to share a break, ranging from 43 to 72
Watts per breath, cookies toasting &
Predicated upon branches, in their buffer being decorated, validated
Against its manuscript's initial flaws
Declare an uneventful decade of boring props, unfinished
       radar prospects
Part of the customer's landslide in metaphor &
Spaces that seal untethered tele-robots, quality ropes, whips, replicas
Of real swimmers, moxie one might fondle even
When the rider is an occasional egg-timer, squandered on a
       rock fixation
& armored against the button, whether or not finite
Rail to rupture the fourth (Critiques on an infinite track, a
       buzzing swarm
Of candles prospecting for wax

100 Most (Female)

V-Thing—Isn't that crazy? A little bit of white, a bit of an edge,
Being touched is refreshing when you don't impress secondary skin.
Where I was crying, at war through moves, teeth fixed, ten years,
"My lucky regimen is effortless," says the doctor we hired.
Wow! Since then, not overly glam, six-minute curling kind of color,
An iron time back in, secret weapon cheerleader! Voluptuous
Impurities aren't always compatible! Bravo pours boobs,
A cannon, namesake perfume! Omigod, tiny! A little junk,
A little carrot juice, lots of water mellows into earthy cream.
Blossoming off the wall is not so great. Spilling happened
To me last week, touching up the game, shrugs, has a fan club
With a large mirror, always looking at the flaws. It must
Have been a battery, take that, without defined eyes, off.
Zoom-in love, no re-touching, chocolaty, messed-up heavens!
Hot is sort of over! Let's cut some bangs! A pushy complex,
Boxes and buns, she's funny, torn-up pretty. Thanks!
Showered, injected, and clean, I'm like a piece of cherry pie:
I can't figure out my sacrifice, what's distributed well!

100 Most (Male)

Away with melting? That's not vanity!
Bring back the spiked hat, razor! A glow,
Whiten them, come quickly the last few months
All right? Anatomy's picked out already—
The same pair of jeans, bobbing for apples
In a volcano. Charcoal circles smudge
The switch—as soft as a nightmare—
The scientific cut—champions of tragedy—
The 11th red paisley. Look: The old hulk
Can still draw a gasp. Plenty prom,
The same formulaic rain. Whatever
Oil's in the cabinet, it's kind of like a runway.
Cheesy but true, I love her butt!
Her butt, her butt, her sleepy butt!
Thirty feet mid-tempo, with diamond,
He's never funky shut into the closet.
A surgeon toy, or bright painting,
Very well, trumps the starched white shirt.

Quatrains in G

That heavily varnished, shiny
Volunteer committee doesn't accept cookies
Crushed in the carousel and explosives
Containing typographical errors

The heroine continually meets and looses
A fire lit in a dance-like atmosphere
Strawberry acres, the brown study, the 24th of June
& marbles rolling around, chains falling on the floor

To select a mirror, convert to the plucker
Thank you for your understanding
No one counts how many you snap
But I like it, wonderful reds

At your door; we offer rests for everyone
That fill the mailing list from day to day
But why does it burn longer?
Roaming memories: Big bang in dark room

Adjusted and checked via time capsule
And to the extent allowed by law
Representing 84 different countries
The quantity of sweet clear you poured

Comfort and quality rooted in tradition
Many modifications of existing lures
The fox is perfect on a tight budget
Stolen camps and festivals, sheets

Nickel plated, nickel silver plateau, .9 bore
With instant "pop," a warm, full-bodied
Branch of air blown across the top
Angle, which is a French word, mistranslated

As a solid silver head for superior warmth
(Our mistakes in filling and/or duplicating)
Find a penpal or information. The message hobbyist
Has a new bore design that integrates vertical

Tunes, three years after he stepped down
What a mystery! It has a pear-shaped
Infrastructure, providing efficient repainting
Of gold/silver plate closed hole models

Or just a passer-by. Hello, null! Having
A moveable U-shaped slide, bent upon itself twice
Something that made a big impression on you?
Including a new version of the star spangled banner

This is incorrect. Dental implants & their
Significance, pedagogy, & performance
By being struck, shaken, or scraped
From each stop and a running

Stick & a practice pad & a rudiment
Further influenced by the enclosed air cavity
Oil soaked despite a sprawling plot
Or balled-up socks sprinkling some salt

Phrenology

It's the new year, so everyone drives in the wrong direction

That their manifestation is innate, as many particular organs

Tracing my fingertip across the lines of your new ink
Disrobed for this purpose from its bacitracin blanket

& just a list for my sake: stars, nipples, phoenix, an anchor
Limited only "mad flow," to suspend or push to the limits

The sky so clear the plane's puffs scrape against it
A radio tower crisscrosses the flight paths of swallows

Rolling lightly and gently enabling you to enclose it
Catty-corner & fold the edges into flexible aluminum

Or a helicopter flying directly at me—ammo pulsing

3 or 4 or 5 or blue, seems to be circling I'm not certain why

An elaborate map: sidewalk, stomach, its shattered windshield
"Wind" in the singular—broken down into its single vectors
Or a partnership with a leaf, relation to its stem's concentric circles

Her rubber factory demoted, a botched witch trial
Its skull's relative development, propensities & faculties

Abduct

You've won our hourly prize
People on the beaches and nearby places
Wheelchair bound in muffet, grabs $50,000
To continue precision incursions, 105
Shit in the head online reservations
Butchered 18 ½ a hike plan start worrying
Rubber chicken, robotic dino, how bad can
This turn? Unlocked, tied up a huge number
The sighting of stamps at a convenience store
Because she was tired & couldn't remember
Wanted false drinking circumstances
A mailbox or a street sign sitting & didn't
Alone in a house. 20 lines noted, muted
The first stage in this sinister journey
With a scar, charged over skirts
Cranberry relents, who put her on a train

Declaration Distilled

One

a a a a a al all an and and and and and and and and and and
and and and and and and as but by by by could could did far
far for for for from from from from from had has has has have
I in in is it it it it it its its its its its like more more most must no
no not of of of of of of of of of of of of on on on our our our
our our own own such that that that that that the the the the
the the the the the the the the the the then this those to
to to to to to to to to to to to to whose whose will will will
will

One-A

all all are are ask bad be bring cease comes date day drive
earth end faith felt few give give grave groups hints hope is
lead lead mass meet peace peace plans put see showed side
source stop strength take there threat threat threat threat
threat threats us us vast want was we we we we we we we
we we we we world world world year years

Two

accept actions actions actions against against ago also any
attacks before better challenge clearly confront country
courage danger deadly defined designs destroy discuss

49

ending entire even events forget gather given human longer minutes never notice oceans only other other others others outlines people present protect recent refuge regime regime regime's required resolve resolved resolved secure seeking shelter sudden support support terror terror terror today today tonight toward tragic vivid weapons weapons weapons weapons witnessed

Three

aggression aggression arises arsenal chemical condition confronting deception defending defiance destruction directly eleven eleven 11th every history history history liberty nuclear possesses practices produces suffering terrorist violence

Four & Up

biological consequences determination development generations obligations responsibilities responsibility terrorism violated vulnerability

Rough Draft

To tuck one's corner into a short stack of graphs
Solace of an empty that radiates asterisks, &
This one peering into 21. An escalator's resolve
To substitute one sculpture for its photocopy.
To color between staff & clef, undoing one
Button at a time, viola's mathematical echo &
Cello's truncated calf. To preponder bees
& cups of grenadine, a little pile of salt
Into which to press your index, dinner's
Skin-taut woodwinds, a persimmon, a calendar.
To scroll again & again, folding cream
Into its crimson parallel, & every to enumerate,
To set fire of its harmonious opaque table
Of contents, titles inscribed across the spine

Notes to Section Two

2.1 With no idea of what to do nightly, the handy stable's a little scrambled.

2.2 Thanks to pep testers, zip dancers, gun trivia, & press boxes.

2.3 Aluminum string is vulnerable to mixed reflectivity wrappers.

2.4 Intrepid apple, bidirectional hat—emits red peaches, forged in ice.

2.5 To transform second stepping circuit, switch stones, rent hot & huge.

2.6 Floppy squid backported to an official freak's bias, handful of cases.

2.7 Slash, scoop, submit fresh meat! Your broken branch is cold!

2.8 My genuine installs your genuine. Four validation manifests.

2.9 Skipping skinnable maturity removes odd amp moisture, crushing oranges.

2.10 Leopard for something like ten minutes, a tiger pond, an engraving system.

2.11 Or, enzymes on the crow's branch—a rapid phosphate.

2.12 Banshee twinkles free games, an audacious snapshot.

2.13 Fried radio episodes on the activities of clumped together pairs.

2.14 The gnomes are stunned, managed by nautilus and asterisk.

Three: Action's Rusty Anchor

So you climb

Up through the chimney to reverse the process brick
By brick and count them study the lines of the bricks
& not just the grid between, they're theoretical
but sturdy enough for a wind-resisting structure
To slide across the surface like a skipping stone
Examining your features in return & start a crop
Of peanuts. Change one into a pet and tie a string
Around & drag it behind you, the sharp edges
Generate tiny sparks & light this notion aflame

Just as you understand yourself to be the meat
Between two loaves & reach for the levers
Of the old motel vending machine, choosing
Between peanut butter for flavor or oil
To reduce friction playing the challenging game
Of trying to match this shape to that space
& this one to that one & this one to that no
Thank you & this one to that one. Because even
Though the wolf is hanging around by the bar top
Three buttons undone & drooling up the starlets
Still the drive both to throw caution & split hairs
To come to some conclusion finally something
About consumption & gestation both & arrive
At the dome at the top & only see Santa
At least that's what you think you see

Action's Rusty Anchor

Breezes the train I can reach I can clip the hedge quickly, the one with whom we are timorous & chafing tuff tonight. Which one's art's? The circle at the end of the lap.

For writing a memo naught error or maybe porch, lights shimmering & on to night's calculation of another & another & read that book an airplane on the top & red like icing. Or it's hour or more for vehicles before the moments are before & just enough evidence (seat on the nose, a Lincoln (should I have been driving three & only when Sam, gas's mooring station for 400 years, I've been telling you that story &, laughing, can't finish

So soft a toddler knocking where am I how did this all come to pass & who drove us all the way here without bouncy something like a witch two counties at once & fuck it, keep the hella way from my property.

No it's not only that & that & really really store) miracle & drive up skydiving's remains sold it for the last one before someone sucked it up on its own belly & held up the flap as if tent were cement & chocolate & damp for opening, its ladybug wedged into its seat, saying it'd rather roses or lettuce or abstraction's mooring, a note to swim yourself up & wear a suit & tie although white is nice this time of year too.

Unicorn Poem for Jessica

It's very horny & pink.
It thinks it might fly, but that's Pegasus's territory,
A fatal mixed myth. For Santa's sleigh runner
Clips the little fella behind the ear,
Opening a gash the shape of a rainbow
& slays the pseudo-horse. All the bunnies
Collect around the corpse & throw daisies
& chocolate eggs. Even the tooth fairy
Takes two teeth.

Self Help

A chicken soup for the rainbow lover's soul.
A chicken soup for the lover of chicken soup.
A carnage of birds, a devastation.
Chicken soup for the dried-up garden—
It's been a lousy summer sucking us dry.
Chicken soup for the grocery list.
Chicken soup for unwanted potatoes.
Chicken soup for extinct animals.

In the west, the sun sets upon chicken soup.
With or without noodles or rice or barley,
Or vegetables—canned or otherwise—
Carrots and celery or egg drop chicken soup—
Chicken eggs, of course—or the alphabet
Or chili sauce. Chicken soup for chili lovers,
For the spicy soul. Chicken butchered
& boiled specifically for your cold.
A chicken soup for the cold soul,
A chicken soup for the sole of your shoe.

A chicken soup for decision making:
Does she love me? Or love me not?
Knots tied with chicken soup.
Chicken soup tied and sold in knots.
38 ways to tie your soup, to be tied.
Chicken soup for the protection of others.

A prayer to chicken soup, may it bring me
A winning lottery ticket. Chicken soup
For recovering alcoholics who still
Need hydration. A hydrangea's
Chicken soup—to be loved like no other.

A chicken soup for Barry Bonds—
May he break Hank Aaron's record.
Stick a pin in the chicken soup & bet
On its opponent. 30-Love. Match point.
A chicken soup for winners.
A chicken soup for losers.
Chicken soup for those who tie or draw.
The 60-plus occupations of soup.
Chicken for Sue, born in the year
Of the snake. The snake that ate
An alligator and died. They both died.

A chicken soup for the one who is eaten.
A chicken soup for the one who eats
Things other than chicken soup.
Transcending the bowl. A meta-bowl.
Chicken soup for the transcended bowl.
Chicken soup for the transcending soup.
Chicken soup for the Marxist, steering
Away from values associated with hierarchies.
Chicken soup for the mud wrestler,
The roller derby queen. Chicken soup
For dairy queen, for the queen of hearts,

For Lady Di and the paparazzi,
For clean and dirty kings and queens,
For kiwis with wings, for the royal
Food pyramid. Chicken soup in
January, it's so nice
To slip upon the sliding ice.

Restaurant

Where it's very easy to get into the wrong line
& queue there & expectant & noisy & the hacking:
A cough, someone trying to get in & adjust the beads
To pop at different numbers—point five green
& one for blue, cone stabilized on its tip
& by the baseline, with vanilla or mint
Diluting into the table's pores. Pass me your fortune
On top of this spoon & embellished by jimmies.
A lobster targets your toe, standing even like snake eyes
Or quad threes as lucky. A starfish's sharp edges
Corner this particular blanket, because the breeze
Is here & strong & dispersing. Whole grain seed.
Picture of a cow in a prospect of flowers. Dalmatian's
Surprising stab at plot—it's a do-gooder, my favorite,
On our ride not only back to the horses, but workbench,
Direct mail, the witchcraft stirring your viscous soup,
Meddling, eleven of them, back in the corner.
We'll always outprice the little one; I've never met
Her before, but see the scripts she reads on television.
Caves where the draft sends her are graciously hurtin' &
A perfect place for giraffes.
Three ice tea & the wave of the future.

Retail Tale

Let's parachute in & give them a big surprise!
In my work line, a soft puzzle's depicted as a rocket—
Unable to be engaged for even a single day,
& a change in flesh—purple skylight impressions—

Or made to reappear as textures, take chairs,
Concerned with raising margins, talking tides,
Specialization, consignment or ground sales, rote
Cannibalization, finding prophet's most direct route

So that I'd be available to decide, know somehow
While misplacing one a dime, come to realize
When the "slow down" sounds of three quarters
Mean a better birthday card or a restless crackle

Mean transportation, or partake in too many things—
Like this one, where the e-technician is correct—
Leading either to a playground or a park to,
If nothing else, redirect several's suspicions

A peach, for example, is an idealistic battle.
To turn time you'll need to be full—
Bringing shrinkwrap, rising crispness—
Where how the West was won, have you any?

Meeting Minnows

1

Whose place indeed?
On this map, everything seems congruent,
A leg up here & an eye down there,
Streams & highways to observe & to which to
Listen. To fold, to nimble, to put
A stamp on it & coast, letting
Edge seem like the end of the world,
A dock to it or barefoot across
Witnesses standing just around
The chain link, one in a hat
Chewing on an apple
& hoping for snow to make
The dots align just right

2

Right now people are finding what they need in the warehouse
Without a requirement to price, display, carry, or abort
& pounding with firsts on the paperclip exterior

Square that shapes it, she's coming to town &
Fixin to share a drink, apartment's small & dusty
& constant, its 1000th book balanced precariously

Atop the glass of seltzer, its fizz a preamble

To millions, debonair & scented of peppermint
Its faucet dripping, granite tarmac, magic square

In which everything in line is good & matches

3

Dirge's cake to eat it too a pylon
Stands between purse
& snatcher, allegorically only
Of course, & rapid enough
To translate into 47 languages what's
The geometric alternative the landscape
That tines the clock?

4

I had a button where my assumption should have been.
Nickel gets you a character coat, an atmosphere.
Typical amphitheater, one that blooms temperature.
A cave & an action. A violence. An imperative.
Twice the allegory that she was, asleep in a balloon.
Where an arsenal divests, pantalooning around its perimeter.
The very aviation of the petal, its posthumous twill.
Moving into an afterlife at a snail's pace, attempting
To salt the hallway for friction, apostle of brine
The conflict of apparent chain, participles extracting
Particular vitamins, A, C, E, O, & vision

In Like an Iamb & Out Like a Line

A string of people playing one another
The giraffe's neck's keys turn tonally higher
As the performer accesses the nape

Fine, extra fine, vintage, mint
& rosemary butter for the freshly baked bread
Syrup on the side because it's sweet & Sunday
& Sunday morning I don't like to eat sweets, just coffee

A drama of two just sitting at a table & talking
After an hour, she reaches & touches his hand, recedes
& grabs the sugar instead, sprinkles it in her coffee

Later, at the zoo, he is particularly attracted
To the African wilderness display, containing three
Elephants, a couple of rhinos and zebras
Much grass & a little stream

My rough-hewn environmental pairings. Knowing
My burning might cause someone else to cough
Or even a stir-fry or overcooked French fries

Coupled with, the voice within the steam
Finally tells me when I walk onto the balcony
I'm the one who will order everyone to return to work
Even though it's a shame we can't enjoy the pleasant breeze

Containing Iron With a Valence of 2

Left your handshake at the door, or rather,
Described the shoes you might take off & socks & stay a while

Even inside toes might print, leaving segments in the snow
Or a grid from a shoe, latitude & longitude
Depending on the angle of your neck

Or email, which is tidier. I have a soft spot
For ice & other winter sports like, uh, curling.

The one that slips and sweeps—the clean one,
Soaped & respectable & shiny & loved.
Even your hair is floral,

Or that's her name—Flora. Flora Nwapa.
Flora fair & faun. Floating high above the fair

It's the ferris wheel, silly. Round like a curling stone
& bristly like a brush, naked as a design
In the foothills of Pennsylvania a bridge builder

Wild eyes & wheels on the brain

Edge

When it voids you can switch power levels and want blackberry detractors, say it's sloppy & founded on unwarranted down. What is never clearly enhanced & used for any packet, spanning rows & columns in search of more flexibility & trying to sneak your way but small? Can rare's sugar sweet take on a gardening sim? They were fighting over a woman in the plane; some 41 rise against the pilots. How is this a stepping stone? Neverending white lights break open a new market for 360 crack on size, this aluminum can stores all the restrictions, tripling the gross robustness. Do lips of an angel hinder your dangerous idea? Assumption's juice? Have adjustability on the fly, my dynamometer.

Level

Extrapolated fabric of the iris
To deliver this perimeter
This pink outline

Parsed according to ancient melodies
Harmonies of & cubed for
Romantic consumption

A carafe of zinfandel pocketed
& folded into a hexagonal
Security blanket

Because the hydrant spews abstractions only
Tape recordings of liquids & steam
Manuscript of an arrest

After an 80-foot marble, volkswagen
Pivoting over its bearings
After a chase down the freeway

& folkways of passenger seats
& familiars of glove compartments
Comfortably nestling & purring its axis

Full of meadow & hump of glass
Wavering spirit unzipped museum
Showing her exhausting navel

Adjustable Island

Betting two owls & a peacock
& several extra fiber optics
Mixed amidst punctuation marks

& all to turn over for a stave
With legs crossed, given in
To the flight risk, to the luggage

Jammed in over the heads, rows
& rows of rooks & knights & pawns
& conflicted dribbling, happy carrot

For a meal or two on wheels
For the door opens & the person bows
& you duck under the spider webs

Careful not to bump your head
& disarm the staircase. For the right
To a foot above the present tense

For the slight disadvantage of having
Ever to look over the shoulder to
See oneself: See, giving those circles

To the extension, unscrewing
The extinguished bulb, gazing between
The parted knees to see what's left lit

& anchor in the fissures to find
The inarticulate cubes beneath, architecture
You always assumed would downstream

& over the rocks, drinkable, to
The idiot lake, because, as wet as you are,
You duck onto an outcropping & make

Smoke & stick to the cold ones
& wonder if any of these echoes
Are really mirrors, and not just

Audio to visual, but a commentary
On light & the future, one you'll be
Screaming to abandon (metaphorical) canoe.

Leaks

Sprung 4, gathering perfect nuances, the scarlet through which all twigs might be woven, amounting to trickles mingling with granite—a type of sheen, unscrapeable, its luster an unexpected phone call—and hang up, dreading an unraveled spoon, one that—mechanized—filters into round & square, soft & long, edible & in, tangles detached or sent, series of unerasable flags. Comb the 7 postures of smoke, the next one designed to navigate backwards from the tangent's fork, toward the navel's inaccess, toward the orange subterfuge, toward the harvest that scales the intestines, toward the ultimate agent of hiccup or tickle or narrow or sudden stabbing. Insert finger, complete the circuit.

Redemption Token

The bird that whistles in your sugar maple
Is a fraud, its song the scratchy fragments
Of a public address announcement, asking
All of us to please move to the front, move
To the front, please. Fire's got
The southernmost outcropping
& pleased as plastic, devours whatever
Sings. Take these seals, for instance.
One dove into the middle of a toy—
Does it have to be a phantom, sending current
Up the wires & toward home, a gothic
Place with rattling chains & demonic
Immigrants? If you have the time
Won't everything eventually
Turn your way, the tide & all
Of the empty spaces: buttonholes
& boxes, stomachs & teeth, awaiting
Fulfillment from a good marketing plan?
In the rising tide, crackles stem
From everything you've dropped.
Touch it & burn but be saved.

Notes to Section Three

3.1 Sticks are easier and more flexible.

3.2 Shrink freezes to find its instant law.

3.3 Amazing volunteers contribute partial regression.

3.4 Acting under paper, you read the salty news.

3.5 A divine monster brings a wave to light.

3.6 The horseshoe's secondary mirror changes focus.

3.7 Nothing but a small trapeze can arm the nurses.

3.8 After folding, take a look at this aluminum spring.

3.9 Thank you to stars for their stuttering rockets.

3.10 An escape sequence has restored a simple null literal.

3.11 A sort-of lightspeed minesweeper of hearts.

3.12 A probable ion succeeds the sixth stone surgeon.

3.13 A ghostly termination of strings detected.

3.14 And they all lived happily ever after.

Four: Unfulfilled Crossword

Deck

The taser of hearts. The pistol of clubs.

>The kwandao of diamonds. The dart of spades.

The fabric of spades. The bolt of hearts.

>The hem of clubs. The button of diamonds.

The spare of diamonds. The strike of spades.

>The split of hearts. The open frame of clubs.

The stop of clubs. The caution of diamonds.

>The go of spades. The yield of hearts.

The clever of hearts. The cunning of clubs.

>The dopey of diamonds. The insight of spades.

The hop of spades. The jump of hearts.

>The skip of clubs. The gallop of diamonds.

The less than of diamonds. The greater than of spades.

>The equal of hearts. The fraction of clubs.

The feet of clubs. The ankle of diamonds.

>The calf of spades. The thigh of hearts.

The dragon of hearts. The minotaur of clubs.

>The basilisk of diamonds. The medusa of spades.

The obsession of hearts. The biscuit of clubs.

>The fawning of diamonds. The terror of spades.

The fewer of spades. The diamond of hearts.

>The clinging of clubs. The heart of the diamond.

The salt of diamonds. The grips of spades.

>The tingling of hearts. The canopy of clubs.

The drinking of clubs. The hot wheels of diamonds.

>The urge of spades. The cleft of hearts.

Unfulfilled Crossword

So bend it happy & reading & sam full of fruit,
The quarter on your belly aches to spend, to
Draw, to divide & weep. So you clean out
The closet & spend your savings on discards—
Bowls of shoes & rackets & outcomes & steer,
The left breaks ranks & shatters conversation
Like a mirror, the last limps clear to the end
Of the vast hall, where a golden doorknob
Jests. Puzzles? Weaving this lace through
The clear square & skip the filled, clear &
Skip, clear & skip, until the heart
You've rendered splats its red across
The just functioning beach, one that substitutes
As a metaphor for the many, grainy shadow
& all. The one that—in all of its glorified swirls—
Approximates a stagecoach, tinkling piano
Invisible in the foreground, & cash lain
To account for it, the one less empty,
The cardboard city full of weeds. Tumbling
Up through the granite clearing, ribs cascade
To inform that someone's underneath, breathe,
Imagine the cumulonimbus storms might
Break this territory in half like stale bread
& put some marshmallow fluff on it

Bats

Not exactly the one you were expecting

A dot, halfway along the box score—fifth?

When the crayon is color; cloud, o, daily, o
Three along the mists of, no, the smudge
Of the times against yr bosom, bleeding its headline
& varicose veins—the one about its prison
& yr superimposed intelligence currency

The nickel redesigned to incorporate the buffalo one final
The nickel redone to Jefferson in profile & to clip, not to
          straight in the eye, no?
The quarter rewritten to incorporate state right—one per
The dollar revamped to stunt, now one'd need special string
          & a harp & an echo &
To reveal under the magic pen, which costs arms & legs

Happy b bonnet 4 & 20 blackbirds baked

Ones that cascade thru the opening, edging 4 yr hair

Dependence

If having another arm would help you.
The thought of carrying you across a trickling stream.
Coming up with the right punctuation.
While driving in circles, a sweaty radio.
Content just to show her nasty legs.
Hoping you'll tell me what you mean by that.
Alarming you with rice, thinking it's never phenomenal.
By passing pipe & exception, an interior protractor.
Or my apple appeal, having thought lips enough.
A couple of figurines, first telephone connection.
Or too much's tone, dessert with me.
A telling piñata, platitude's full-sail exception.
Plus the hustle factor, 2 eggs & only 1 spoon.
Giving rise to clementine's clever current.
A parcel in a pear tree, an enveloping exchange.

Meaning

An unexpected rivalry between east and west

Untangling the balloons from the banana tree limbs,
One never before inhabited and barely enough to hold
Falling down a story or through another character's window

Meeting you in a hat on block, passing

The duotone tattoos—crows and leaves—
Decorating your breasts and neck

Four-fold toy contests—which is the best metaphor?—
But unexpectedly rigged
Sex in a car, a phone booth

Or someone thinking, how couldn't rich win,
A troupe of dancers from Singapore
Nine melting candles on a bench
Outside an exclusive club
Look in & see the baseball player

Its shower, the kids running in circles
& angry that you picked someone else
& angry that she too picked someone else

Compare

Losing the page made orthodoxy clamor.
Ten vital signs is more than nine.
Armor becomes you and your tinny reflection.
At the center of the cup is the core of the drink.
To exit means applying one's stop philology.
A compartment for salt, a compartment for silver.
I've brought a dime for the baby.
Its little ego is awash with the pins' vibrations.
An angel divests herself of her toast.
Betting on the quarter-horse instead,
A breakfast of champions pings its united segments.
That is, to align the trajectories of returns.
Making a solid of the playing field, or its atmosphere.
It's hard to breathe in the rain, the telephone one.
The characters for metal & divine are equal.
The light at the end of the tunnel is a limit,
Always to approach and never to attain.
Those who follow the vacuum believe in mixing.
Mapping an alphabet doesn't mean a set.
To make the most efficient path a circumstance.
Cast iron's vehicle, steering obstacles astray,
Assigning subdivisions to water, a net
To reign in the apples, spiders
To capture the molecular of

Juxtapositions

I.
vanilla, vuh-NIL-uh or often NEL-uh, n., adj., the extract of
this seedpod, the bean of this orchid. Its synthetic flavoring
agent. We went through a period of vanilla cars. Of ordinary
sexual preferences. Macerated in alcohol, its fleshy leaves,
white or vanilla or topaz climb the version. Diminutive of
the vagina. The notion of whiteness. To orthogonalize chip
nomenclature, for instance, hot-and-sour soup. Along the
sidewalk, each movement is a fragment of vanilla against the
street's ice cream.

II.
cube, kyoob, n., v., a universe's outmoded representation, the
measure of a combustion engine's flashcube. To tenderize
a slice of meat by scoring the fibers in a pattern. I've three
calculators in my cube. Planes interpenetrate to create
the shallow, ambiguous space. Still life with fruit dish and
mandolin. Any of several tropical, woody plants, whose roots,
nonmetallic and cleavable, somewhat lustrous, form calcite
veins. In this otherwise empty grid, what intends the single
opaque cube?

III.
seed, seed, n., v., adj., not to be confused with comets,
whose tails might tangle. A small bubble in a piece of glass,
produced by defective firing, to scatter with silver iodide
crystals. What you saw: a lake with trout, an icy bridge with

chemicals, rankings by team or talent. In tennis, gone to seed
over the past few years. What had meant fruitful now means
shabby. The sea men sowed sunflowers, removed them
from grapes or pits from cherries. A silkworm lands on a nut.
Attested from 1933, the field.

Hiding Places

A hollowed-out cantaloupe

A hollowed-out doorknob

A hollowed-out bullet

A hollowed-out doughnut

A hollowed-out mudslide

A hollowed-out air freshener

A hollowed-out needle

A hollowed-out ice cream cone

A hollowed-out pen

A hollowed-out crayon

A hollowed-out kimono

A hollowed-out porcupine

A hollowed-out pond

A hollowed-out belly

A hollowed-out snowball

A hollowed-out sandwich

A hollowed-out faucet

A hollowed-out can-opener

A hollowed-out sheet

A hollowed-out syringe

A hollowed-out citation

A hollowed-out dictionary

A hollowed-out turkey

A hollowed-out sunbeam

A hollowed-out washer

A hollowed-out dryer

A hollowed-out syllable

A hollowed-out septuagint
A hollowed-out excuse
A hollowed-out phone
A hollowed-out daydream
A hollowed-out departure

Top:

It's on the tip of my tongue, and not necessarily a word.
Creamier than the moistest of phonemes, even "sh" or "l"
Pales in comparison. The moon reflects in far fewer pixels—
What? The image isn't clear. It's red, of course, & subtle.
Or was that supple? As wet as freshly laid paint or polish.
More pliant than an apple, subdivided for additional accuracy.

Down:

Strawberries might be artificial, but the whiff of you
Gives them true bite. You add an extra element to each knot.
Not? An open o, becoming long, yes, but still, at the moment
Clipped, & flirtatious in that. As in "owl." Or an intruding t,
But not a towel or something to drink. A consonant blend
Is the mixing of bodies and dreams; a vowel blend is liquid.

Irrigate

Bend it to get a better angle
Across your knee, what you saw
Through dirigible's sky

The part that turns in
A kaleidoscope's current
Wing that west & change

For dime's ablution. Regulation?
Bend to access the section
Around its corner

The copper piece bronze braid
& your stiff lip to encase it
Seeing who has to

Gather everyone into a room
& review who died & why
How's thunderstorm

Or wagon wheels
Redistributing gravel. Couple
Holes, a creature

Wriggles its ends & parched
Awaits atmosphere's
Hydrogen reallocation

A paper one, an airplane's
Worth of moisture that flutters
To the stem

Too late & paused for instruction

Means

1. Animal

tubes		rhapsody		choose		pencil		letter	
	string		adding		smoky		muddle		rummage
quartet		variable		rolled		wedge		scramble	
	range		comes		tactic		gesture		phantom
climb		cherry		region		sweep		locomotive	
	spoon		stuff		pilot		warmup		alloy
tongue		motion		boom		zipper		cathode	
	swallow		visual		carnival		faster		copper
zigzag		factory		hoist		streaming		cluster	
	spoil		horizontal		buckle		domino		phase

2. Vegetable

shipped		fluffy		along		silver		stirring	
	nesting		instant		spanning		spoon		square
handler		protocol		quiz		merge		measure	
	hook		white		revert		zoo		starch
root		nickel		dance		ogle		stapler	
	breast		percolate		clover		flag		cotton
tart		bolster		lines		mystery		vibrant	
	vanilla		bridge		solstice		crime		complex
licorice		slide		basin		gate		margin	
	thistle		sediment		scoop		circuit		proof

3. Mineral

various	forbidden	wedding	symmetry	refract	sheets	drilling	shallow	plotted	slew
nestle	bubble	aromatic	audible	duplicate	volume	spill	needle	spherical	smatter
plume	ratio	burning	ventilate	azimuth	aviation	region	spool	remnant	enigma
school	vinyl	tilt	voltage	quarter	speed	engine	alter	flexible	spring
cabinet	level	screws	titanium	junction	tectonic	passage	bleeding	snare	emerge

4. Other

blue	spike	clean	cross	vestment	divine	ankle	stream	fluid	undress
unending	wholly	ambrosia	chestnut	race	tie	duress	limp	stutter	waves
open	irrational	ramble	chariot	pox	strain	aggress	surge	flutter	protract
erupt	flow	interrupt	stricken	fall	epidemic	recover	sine	reticent	withdraw
project	up	height	stop	segment	winter	element	hermetic	singular	since

Definitions

1. To gaze, retract, and subsist only on carbonation
2. At the end of a long day, to imbibe, to mock orange
3. To abdicate all surviving matter; to vacuum annihilation
4. See also knot; to pretend pig for the purpose of absolution
5. To vote on whether or not to vote; to tie an untieable clean
6. To Freud & to Jung, to Adler, Klein, or Horney
7. To match a strike in the pins of maze and made
8. In food preparation, to construct butterflies from carrots
9. To fluster by talking incessantly about genitalia
10. To park on a decline, for instance, one's sport utility vehicle
11. To deceive by calling, "Caw, caw; I'm a crow!"
12. To remain motionless while the surrounding cement laments
13. To be bricked into a wall while clutching a cask of amontillado
14. In basketball, to hang on the net until the backboard shatters
15. To refrain from smoking, drinking, dancing, or hopscotch
16. To prefer thick fabrics, including leather and velvet
17. Every other weekend, to worship the neverending lines
18. To pack sausage into parallel densities, one visible
19. To pocket the three in the omnivorous corner
20. To dust with the expectation of umbrella
21. To dictate one's skeleton to the annals of tape
22. To deflect and chew the gamey library
23. And aftermath, to fledge & bowl sublimely

Circles

...s, unc...
...a was that the sou.
, hand built this huge w
:k, so too does atmosphei
ary maintains the Circle N
iduals, groups, networks,
e world. Every thing lo
's, spreading its little
"ght. This in'

.. the .
ues, the pres
1 short video r
'y, could repe'
'ds is bet'

...
showing h.
ns spiritual p
·de or implie
'ance—

...
with their typic.
, a segment, radically .
.1 are considerable and th
w each other. The man fir
ïlls the sky. Politely carry
'atter. We appreciate the
'opment of least restr'
"ding the dile"

...sposed upo..
.ised shadow. We belie
.gh age eight are at a formati
od! how final! how it puts a nev.
s past the fountain, electing not to
oral-philosophical, and research b;
models for young children with di·
·arel became blanketed with silt,
by that which follows. Electi·
·r gathered backwards. Li'
'ıd every dew drop
'. ·on +·

,ourney
,oon gets wo
ıd presently, ;
ious ladder '
·nsio·

Flat: Sentences from the Prefaces of 14 Science Books

1. Mary-Frances applied continual pressure on me to start the job and helped in recording and editing.
2. Thanks to Sandra for her heroic typing, although this need not be taken to indicate her agreement with various points.
3. Peter provided information about the notorious perpetual pills.
4. As someone who gloried in seeing dogma overturned, he would have delighted in the irony of seeing arguments for the reverse.
5. And without their willingness to take on the chore of responding to our whims and fancies over a 3-year period, this book would have fallen short of its goals.
6. The production of this tome would have been unthinkable without the marvelous electronic tools that are now widely available.
7. However, Chapter 7 was written in a relatively self-contained fashion, so the serious student may skip Chapter 6 and delve directly into the theory.
8. The late abbess of Shasta Abbey proved that looking through different windows into the same room is not a metaphor.
9. Nick, who is writing a book on oxygen, gave much appreciated data concerning that element.
10. The filmstrip format employed in Chapter 10 originated with Elizabeth.

11. I have been very fortunate in being able to use such penetrating minds.
12. In recent months, I have often felt like a small child in a sweet shop as astronomers all round the world have sent me the most mouthwatering new data.
13. Suffice it at this point to observe that I am not just talking about wallpaper patterns on shirts and dresses, although many of these patterns do turn out to have interesting properties.
14. I do not expect that many readers will want to be masochistic enough to want to read the book in order from cover to cover.

Notes to Section Four

4.1 Pink rails, left, right, & center, ruby citrus, wanting pool

4.2 Threaten cinema diesel, cinnamon engines, manual glow

4.3 Shall solicit citations, the duplication of raw desire

4.4 Bondage in between a film—can she cascade?

4.5 Needles on fire to cross off my list, half pattern

4.6 The exception handler has a simple name & face

4.7 Turbidity in body, in surface—peach references

4.8 Or repeating horny propellant, a first look at your shoulder

4.9 Lying down, side by side, top to bottom, digital bagging

4.10 Edgy is what most people want—multicore & torrent

4.11 Framed in steel beams & tangled in pipes, conduits, & coils

4.12 It's the last accident, valentine, exploding on the launch pad

4.13 The chance, my meteor, to rule with fingerprints

4.14 Slicing operator syntax, unpacked arrays, an empty queue

Five: Urge

Urge

Your soft breath a school, and to look for the eyes of it
The altitudinal lines of it, the railroads and bike paths of it
Through the nest of wires, casings shaven to expose
The reflective copper of it, pushing the light off schedule
& in the waiting room with a newspaper & next to
A 34-year-old blonde with a broken ankle, reading
About the storm of it, trees encased in an inch of ice
Branches crumbling—an application of whole grain cereal
Sickles and milk, your sheepish glance but sentenceless
Tapping your toes against the edge of the glass table
The restless vertex of it, a function of cigarette moistened
In turns by your lips, the inquisitive roots of it, clinking
Against the peripheries, the need to replenish after
A run on its inventory, an awaiting stick of it jittering
An awaiting bar of it, a plastic box keeping it
Distanced from its expiration date, the dirty clumsing
Of it, fumbling with transparent, tiny buttons
One at each word's deliberate interval, the navigational
Steps to absorption, waiting for the lightbulb to crack
& plant its little seeds & grow new ones clamoring
To be the first to switch. Instead, I bought you
A succulent for it, needing only a needle's eye
Of water each day, less even than a tuber, a canary.
The tracing of the landscape of it, suspecting
Someone's behind your back & stealing
A paperweight, gold hurricane in the middle

Wiggling its tendrils & laying waste to the under-
Burdened, with a clock on its size & bearing
These fragile clusters, ready to pop
Their packets & bawl for frilly subliminals

Body & Isn't

I have a hard time making my mind take place.
Every input adjusts the chemistry—water, peppermint stick, analogue.
Kisses are circles. With eyes closed, every taste buds almond orange.

Ceiling defines the segment; door, the vector. Exits & entrances.
My location's ribcage is beneath the changing spectrum's breast.
Heft of a wet peony, white & pink, drips its honey south.

Conducted back, your body accelerates—biology of a taxi ride.
Kept kempt, migraines at bay, tidy nails, & sneezes away.
Sex through collisions—bridges jumped & limbs tangled.

Or the chromatic staff arranging the spheres' accidental spills.
Frets & intonations strung across a tempered series of knots,
Strung through the loops of our virtual displacement.

But it isn't wings or hooks or hooves or horns or see-through or white.
Whether afloat in a boat or aloft in a plane. The way maps affect time.
For a second I think I feel the fleeting texture of your skin.

Lumbar & sacral nerves descend to exits beyond the end of the cord.
Keep the blood in at all costs, even when the wind crackles its cells.
The coming of electricity, half next time & half this:
My five. My unending ache at the absence of you.

Look, No Hands!

Tomorrow: It's a song washing through, redirecting each junction
Or: Pressing the braille until it ruptures, suffocating
Ten burrowing rabbits underneath its stairs

For example, the first time: You answered rain definitely
I'm on the couch: Coupling across the woof
How does your garden grow? With silver bells & cockle shells

Or rows of mirrors: Foil & window clung according to static's laws
Sudden shape, snap to grip, thinking a lode of diamonds
Marry the walls, its grassy field admits the game, administers

Shuddering. & bolt all the apertures, orifices, & mouths
Lapping up the soda drops, fizzy & wet & strawberries
Holding down mine, ten of them tied, casting

Its other side fortune: Lucky roll, a sculpture, perfectly
Embossed screw, cards as a function of your core,
Apple, huge push, assembling a chorus of the tracks

But we've hidden in the tunnel's muddy sidebar, cleft
Impression in the granite: Cracked, however, like the
Liberty bell—let's retain its shape just because it's nice

Combustion scent—time to grow from glowing. I see,
When you stopped, surprised, that passing one
Straight thru the other, ionizing, averaging their minerals,
Might just be the only way to seek stripes & frolic

Condiments

My, aren't we the lucky ones?
We've seen pennies, picked them up
& all the day we fucked and fucked.

A candy cane's anima is the number nine, welcome
Spoken not only by waiters
But by dishwashers and silverware.
If you do spill salt
Pop & believe, set the island's central fire
On blocks & change its tire.

Isn't alphanumeric, after all, the sexiest position,
Laying claim to whatever is prime?
Fine-tuning the fork! The fork?
Pitch or in the road? Has it resorted to that?

Sure Egypt's a place I'd like to visit!
I brought a lunch full of pasta
That oops I forgot to cook,
The diplomatic counsel divided according
To those who prefer mustard
& those who would rather not pepper

Many's a microboxtop
And exo-proofofpurchase
Intera-rebate and extracollection

One's the font size
Tumbled with salad & arrest,
Let me peel you an orange

Does this flirtation

The nature, crack, & silence bringing lettuce's heart out
Extra's funny way to the shoulder try. By the gulley, side

Of the road, the nice it's clean & slippery bath (on the floor
Now upstairs where "just getting ready for you to pass")
& get-town's high powered firm—no, not like sponges—

Looking out onto the booths again, two piles of leaves,
Are you sure tidy on the sail is peeling?

Can we remember the festival cooked all the way thru
& waking in the night to your scary, first part of celery

Tender's cline to accept the hit without being
Gored? Very, very: A stable, rub the nose &
All of the way to the right—why not just, no I'll

Even before the traffic flows keep me backpeddling
Even though nice they're very & various nice

Soda Pop Girl

For 22 pennies the female version rites
Cover flower, smoke, fierce of body.
Spurii's conceptual thread, a prosthetic battle,
Come whatever rode. Forks left to right.
Coaxes across the flash. What is metaphysics?
A butterfly portal snaps instructions
& all variant comb. Twin titles, audacious
Cherry bomber, jumper, torsion breaks
While walking, fee-nom-e-nol wide shut.
A gauntlet's blooming magnet stacks fruit
& swimwear. Take brandy, sitting in
An accident, packed in a regular pattern:
The bright communication hub, three
Addictive waves, round tools, & checklist
More a reckless center. This hardened steel
Will not lose its edge under impact.
Extract area's hazel residence episode.

The Difference Between Toggle Bolts
& Molly Screws

It's like the atlantic around here—jittery &
Full of waves, a desperate need for a horizontal
& vertical juxtaposition, a corner, a vantage point
A start. And if that weren't enough, this device

I found to fasten, without a clear understanding
Of what in the hell needs fastening. Except
I do this: press gently through your center
Nestling, mixing into your microcosmic control

Until its wings finally cross the cusp, detach,
Unfold again on the opposite side, drawing me
As close to you as relative density might allow,
Clinging from the rear of your ribcage

And imprinting according to this grid:
Every minus to crease a plus, every plus
To upend a many a minus. There's a message
Nestled in between us like a traffic signal

Composed of half a dozen buttons & a rook:
"Declining to hear the city's solving tools,
They, in a methodical approach to the construction
Of peculiar fields & frames, dusting full force, yield

Two outcomes, Phoenix on the left, trajectory
From concept to completion on the other,
Redirected to circles, one in my very backyard,
The other spread along every sort of continent."

The process of the phonologically sequenced paper
Or your physical form, a thirdness, where order
The first, trace to follow up your spine & amidst
Your hair an intended & immediate kiss

Second & nonrepresentative because
The moment this is, it is, and then one more

Sonnet

I found a slice in the ice big enough to fit my notes & me.
Why argue over whether to punctuate with a question mark or clef?
Two slices of bread nestle into the staff's spaces & toast.
A future buttered surface flutters vibrato, asparagus
Out-reeding the whistle. When the cord broke,
The baby began to float, catching a diaper pin
Finally on the edge of a cloud. Although the little one
Might cry, at least there's chocolate in this merry-go-round
To settle jangling nerves—a sine-wave type of harmony.
An arpeggio current traps a single shoe on a little
Disappearing island, ruffles a poking crab.
A long line of iron legs—if this ocean's a map—
Divides what's naughty & nice. Or the implied red
Between your lips—what thirsty is & isn't.

Typography's Vestige

Not just the core but the tips of its petals
The one that gathers the one that gathers it
Gathers, coalescing from the sparsest of sketches
Or the one in which every *and* implies a predicate—
Static's prickly community behind glass—
Partly a channel & partly a volume
A cup, a teaspoon, an ounce

The window shatters from the point of impact out—
It's a sun!—crackling its maze, its web of
Sharp, arbitrary orbits—either way the ice
Gives way & the skaters fall under
But make love in the freezing water—in which
Every motion slows & matters

The first time I felt compelled to swoop
It was a quarter to four—the most
Meticulous snowflake—light's morse code—
the pitter patter of rays, broken yet
Sequential, a thermos full of each
& every intersection

Or more, dramatically, my hands guiding your hips

The time we pressed together through

Impressing letters upon the paper

Break or Thaw?

If a team of you became a team of me,
Yes, you'd know then what I'd been thinking
Dogsleds and all, desire to sculpt you
In ice or see your eyes immortalized in glass.
The slick surface of that moment
The way the coating brightens every shade
& polarizes: Red to green; blue to orange;
Buttons to hooks & edges to seams.
& if a whip I do carry, let it be
To drive that device up, up, & over
The crescent of the forthcoming hill
The sun so bright it melts it all to sleep

Electrical Repairs

6 inches of wall with wire snaking in the core
& nestled by foam insulation. It wishes
To sleep, let it sleep. It's too busy, it fizzles
At the very thought of you reading, you
Shaving the peels off of apples, you
Trying to pick up a pin with tweezers.
Look, the air has it. Lend me your ears.
With all the barbs between things
(Kelvin's knot theory regained)
The more you split into cubes at the very
Thought, like on graph paper,
The greater the merry slope. But why
Such a gap? Are even the theories now
Reading? & four more flavors to erupt
Pushing nuts & citrus & florals?
8 versions of plaid, a plaid is a plaid
& the pallid appetite, a chilly archetype,
Shatters in its wake. Tie the shoes.
One can't simply dismiss the arrow
Between A and B; for every action
There's a fuzzy mean occurring
In the second head, just as the lightbulb
Pops open over the first
& slides into home.

Check Box If Deceased

& in doing so, construct a corner to the end
From which to construct a tower then & tower later
Gracious rescue a ladder fire fallen dragon an apple pie
Is freshest when you've just picked them
From dotted trees & peanut butter sandwich stands
Nutrients for the cell your captivity in taxes & fall
& by foot & ain't able to get nowhere

If you screw around in this turret the battleaxes
Will come & leave you throatless   You could
Scale down those vines or the rope there & with vitamins
Just walk down the side ready to be swarmed by
Autograph-seeking bees, eating the fresh pollen
From the apple blossoms, smelling like apples
If only you could smell that small & quick an action

& Toto too grabs you, points out the tin man
Reconstructed as an ice box & keeping the pie chilled
& the heavy cream to go on top with time stopped
& the heavy rain is shimmering globes around him
He reflects the sun through drops tiny rainbows
Filled in soap bubbles his axe poised to split
Them all into hemispheres, tiny ups & downs

& when the dotted earth finally gives leave for cylindrical
Stacks of coins to sprout up in stalks & tiny hands

Reaching, palms up, to collect & incorporate the suspensions
Compounding interest in the letters e pluribus unum
& screaming on the uppermost floors afraid of heights
& too far up to jump   you, like it all, wish to travel
With the smoke of the blown candles wishing

This fabulous birthday wasn't someone else's last

Diptych

To be sure "licorice" is my last word
I'll keep saying it over & over
Until someone shoots me in the face

To ensure the sky will be blue for you
I'll hire all the two-seaters in the world
& tie crepe paper to their tails

Foreign Objects

Hemlock is high in soluble fiber.
A self-directed bullet contains no fatty acids.
Asphyxiation eliminates 2nd-hand smoke.
Carbon monoxide is nitrate-free.

Sleeping pills reduce the body's need for sugar.
A blow from a sword is high in iron.
Hanging flushes the body of its toxins.
Cyanide cleanses potentially harmful resins.

Bleach cuts cholesterol levels.
Jumping simulates weightlessness.
Drowning ensures hydration.
Smoking improves eyesight.

An oncoming train is filled
With many fruits and vegetables.
Running a car into a tree reduces
The need for red meat consumption.

Notes to Section Five

5.1 Will tradition's tablet be washed & pushed?

5.2 Will oxygen's dashboard bury wine's patch number?

5.3 How many blades to secure thunderbird's spill?

5.4 What ghost exports woolen paper?

5.5 When dancing's handy, do comic girls invite?

5.6 The ocean's 5-second thumbnail? Flower monsters?

5.7 Does a spotted rumor groom cheetah's orange?

5.8 The vast majority of heart-pounding slippers?

5.9 Who leaves her comfy chair in support of public safety?

5.10 Whose firewater is cramped & shady?

5.11 Surprised at the malformed mousewheel, Mercury?

5.12 The freezing resilience of the sheer lime skin?

5.13 Frost or torrent situated in liquid typesetter ecstasy?

5.14 Deeper cuts, sugar, come into my heart?

Six: What's Yours?

Jump

An airplane is such an awkward and untidy thing
In disharmony with the runway down upon which it cracks

Or the section of street under shadow
Wearing out more quickly that way

Even the sun sluggish in this cold, cherry syrup for, pinned
To the shoulder, upstate NY now, bales to push
Against your thigh, or looking up & seeing tracks
From all-terrain conversations, in handcuffs
Or galvanizing every edible, particularly organic ones

An astute suggestion, press arm, wrap around shoulder
Clutch round that might dematerialize, solid to liquid

Or rating the brush, strike unwound, pass south
Through your hair, thinking the right time
For a traffic light or overlapping vowels
Bisecting time or fruit, your orange, your pineapple,
Your currants, starfruit, persimmon, lychee

Or standing with toes dangling over the corner
This motion's temperate, clear, undivided, geometric

In the fine grain of this hour

Carved out of the spirit of the tuber
Saline designed to shrink & magnetize gulls

There's one shaped like a fan by that outcropping
& a dead one, fur packed in ice, transpired
By syndicating gnats & oranges

A crystal for someone who doesn't believe in being healed
A chakra mumbled in absent throes

For this bluffing grass, ribcage collapsing & caught
On film, a fractional rowboat labeled "primary,"
Escape to the nth, & at harmony with the jellyfish
In the bay beyond its granite

What either embraces or repels one foot
Before nine, windy, the key's soaked, an empty chair

& eating away, staggering fact of lunch again
After all these years, fighting to push
Your tiger face first into the glass

& shatter into hypotheses, the ones, Janus-
Like, sucking penny to ear, sideways & hyper-vigilant

My first poem in a month is for you

It's been cold here & full of echoes

My too-quiet rings damp; your cotton
Isn't a conduit, or amidst too many shoes
Or books or underneath the ironing board

Or a side door wiggling shut, opaque & seamless

To try even a radio tomorrow?
Its thorny interruptions might hinder
Even a breeze, marbles, folding one
Over the other over the other, but tight & tight
Desire to shift into a higher aching gear

& pass the butter or sugar, a lump
That tells time, drags certain consequence in
Only to realize it's one book in a warehouse of millions

The one you dust off will change your life

Thinking you'll discover or be discovered here

If it's a lake you want, click here!

A beautiful opposite underneath the carousel, the only place we could find.
Or: Lodes of silver & bamboo—put in front of a panda & see if it eats.

Seriously, I'm tired of being pushed. Or pushing because the tire's flat.
Pump it up manually—sure, you might be able to do it better or easier—
Then drive it north to ice. 1000 people tell me where to stay.
Including you. Or grapes eat. With that spoon. A proper distribution.

I tell you I love you and you tell me that's nice. I think, yes,
In front of the subway doors it might be nice—a saxophone playing
& unable, though we see each other's lips moving, to speak.
I'm thinking yours is of paper airplanes, the best way to fold,
& mine is of marbles, the best way to shoot & click & cats-eye.

Thank you, that's very nice.

Particle Distribution

Although I do love, there's a blur when it comes.
Though red and blue together
Create a perception of depth, studies show
Subjects tend to choose either L or R.

Stuck at seven, pointillism is a two-dimensional field
& absorbs time & motion: My assembly of pretzels
Each armed with cubes, the facets of which point.

"Its gelatin silver overlap, a red box,"
A conveyor belt brings them to us.
When the movement's constant, does its shadow too?

Or ferns' shady plot—soil that's electable
& unexpected fragile, a consumer's paradise
Coming up snake-eyes?

It might be folded over, but I've vouched
For its diplomacy, clarity, & flexibility.
My, aren't we that to which
Statistical arrays never seem to stick?

Good & Plenty

At the grocery I order a pound of meat, twice the normal
We have guests who eat meat, coming to visit tonight

At the gas station I let it spill all over:
Me, the sidewalk, the car door & tires

Where you can buy herbs that stay awake all night
& watch the moon drive half circle
& stars so orderly positioned

I pick up Koch's "A Possible World"
I pick up Notley's "Disobedience"

Because blue is too corporate & predictable
This tasty pastry is not predictable

Where cream flows over the top & top
Becomes coffee, grains with which to read futures

& growth hormones & stockings stocked on shelves
By stock women, who rustle in & out of loading

Tugging to keep the awful manager off his knees
& cardinal at the feeder—the sunflower must have

Attracted, its poles (north/south) are
The only fertile & bearing crop locations

Love Poem

I bought you a whole box of grey area
It's what we swapped in for what was rancid and what was sweet

The kite you boarded on a quest for the origins of climate
The woody roots of lightning, thunder's frequency

Ratio of wave to hair, it's curling, swept
With a red breeze, taken as wet communion

Or domino's temperature, suddenly wholly susceptible to gravity
& plummet directly earthward, combustible middle

Day-to-day service re-scripted as a movie review
4 stars 2 thumbs up, restless to wrestle, miraculous lettuce

Ballooning above its tiny legs, let us
Find a river between these two slices of bread

A metaphor for conception, commencement
Or (choose your condiment)?

You Were Wearing

Clavicles percussion ting, a punctuation mark

Heroism's balloon—saving pressure, preparing
For a target, an eighth note, exposed navel

Or: In peeling the orange, moving even the film
Around the dozen-odd wedges, each capsule's bag
Akin to the grains, rice-size flowing thru my wrist
Which except for you I'd split into hemispheres

Is it good to live in the north? Surely, here,
All the bowling balls arc much more true
& not just because the gutter guards are up

But this room—the one we're in now—is special
7% bleeding from a limb, saving the most dire
For a trip to the basement, seeing if everyone'll
Stay seated long enough and imaginary ice man
Slicing past on his mega-track, first time for everything

& knowing, come fall, his antics won't be worth a nickel

Lanes

When, as unhealthy as it might seem, you clarified the axis
& broke the butter along its fault. It's happier the wrong way
With traffic lights designating verticals & horizontals & cease
& flow. This garden is divided into the edibles & the nots
Even, left, among the silvers & golds, the groundcovers
& perceptions of something either tingling or ticking

& when the siren sounds & everything is in the rearview
Backward & closer than they appear with creamy san-serifs
Stretching across the bottom, little alleys to spin a ball through
& see which fortune emerges, I love you. You walk to secure
An extra pair of chopsticks & little more gingerale, east
Among rows & north among columns, the fountain

& the hope of an epiphany bestowed, bubbles zigzagging
Amidst what's true & what might have been

Or Telegraph Cargo

Five times the number of stations, ten times
The number of stops & checkpoints, places
To buy peanuts & candy & coke. I've
Peppermints & popcorn in my pockets.
When I pass any one to you, we brush.
The rope around your wrist isn't just decoration.
At 5:30 pm we're instructed to proceed,
Tickets in hands, to the dinner car.
We see the snowflakes we're leaving
Behind in the preceding counties. &
The lightning that strikes too late
The past's meat & bread & vegetables.
It's a two-way street—well, at least
A split between those who insist on facing
Forward and those who don't mind
Looking back. A dead raccoon, close
To a billion pebbles, the bear 2 miles
Too far from the raccoon, & at least
A dozen frozen silver dollars, or at least
That's what I would have put on the tracks
If the string from this soda can reached
All the way back to when I was ten

Still

No it couldn't have been that long
He died 35 years ago
Some of these buildings weren't even conceived then

But in their drafts, cement corners
Have room for buried secrets
Messages through to center

As we crane our necks to watch them swoop
Just past our noses & from the dimmest
Of dusty starts   Do you believe in long odds

Ever reaching fruition? If so,
Do you have a dime? I need to make a call,
Buy tickets, tea to read the leaves,

& shake my die
Or hope so peacefully
In a quick bluebird's belly

Heal, sort of

& waiting for the contract's dust to clear:
It's projected onto this screen, & although
Black & white, lovely enough to eat off of the floor
To send to your grandmother in lieu of flowers
To speak to apostles left and thin

Universal cleft in the rock, the feeling that,
No matter which channel, it's all about sports
Or a mirror's carefully aligned narrative

The one that's my room, carried off into
Right field where the strong arm
Anticipates the grass's next. Funny
How an aspiration means up, inhaled,
The record of those who wish to have been kept

Standing still in line at the restaurant
& eyeing the door

Thinking ultimately someone will have to pin it back on

What's Yours?

It is about daisies, yes, and narcissus
& iris & the fallen cherry petals
Cascading across the grass like snow.

I just wish, for once, that underneath was
Only a series of horizontals & verticals,
With a little dot in the center of each square,

Rather than these 30,000-ton prickly atmospheres
Poking their way between each blade
& aerating the flesh, thus initiating

The final degradation. My superpower
Is the ability to stop time. My limit is
I can only use it once.

Quantities

Are there more sand grains or bacteria cells?
You'd know, if they hadn't invaded & overtaken
Your lungs. The Flash could move through walls
By vibrating faster than sound & slipping between
Molecules. When not a matter of life or death,
An estimate might make better use of time
In the gauge of matter—How many seconds you
Might have left, for instance, or the strength
Of the push of blood or percentage of O_2
Or other. How much the odds are against death
Ever occurring—can only happen each in one way once.
If you swim & eat your vegetables, will lightning
Be close or far? How many benzene rings
Did it take to unscrew a light bulb? Or, if projected
Onto a screen, what magnitude & number
Assigned to focus—in other words, will you
Stay at least until I finish this single hamburger?

Notes to Section Six

6.1 Three speakers across the front with a sixth channel in the rear.

6.2 Zone objects with methods to manipulate time & memory.

6.3 Uncertain horizontal body, did you feel it?

6.4 Queuing magnitude, a powerful planning cube, chaste island.

6.5 You are not gold? Evolution is the answer.

6.6 Text soap makes it easy to clean invisible characters.

6.7 The last 8-30 days, fast moment green feed damage.

6.8 According to special congestion, intensity of travel stations.

6.9 Or the latest ultra, skinniest, crazy resin snapping helplessly.

6.10 The bluest fashion rubber, gambit & siren notes.

6.11 Tactical pants (unhemmed), reversible rain.

6.12 Direct invocations of arbitrary length speed up the build.

6.13 Scaled according to the ample catalysts of the mountain.

6.14 Magnesium might burn, but I'll try not to.

Acknowledgments

Many thanks to the editors of the following journals and anthologies, in which many of these poems first appeared: *Aufgabe, Bird Dog, Caffeine Destiny, Cimarron Review, Coconut, Columbia Poetry Review, ElevenEleven, EOAGH, Fascicle, 50/50, The Holiday Album: Greeting Card Poems, Horseless Review, The i.e. Reader, Jacket, LIT, Lungfull!, Magazine Cy Press, Melancholia's Tremulous Dreadlocks, MILK, MiPOesias, MiPOesias print, My Friends, New South, 1913, No Tell Motel, OCHO, One Less: Film, Otoliths: Poet-Editors, Parcel, Parthenon West Review, Past Simple, Ping Pong, Saint Elizabeth Street, Sawbuck, Siren, Small Town, Sonora Review, Verse, Wildlife Poetry.*

Three of these poems also appeared as the limited edition chapbook *Three Poems* (Ready Set Readings).

Texts from "100 Most (Female)" and "100 Most (Male)" come from *People* Magazine. "Declaration Distilled" reorders the first and last two paragraphs of George W. Bush's non-declaration speech of war on Iraq. "Circles" includes some sentences from Emerson's essay "Circles."

About the Author

Bruce Covey lives in Atlanta, Georgia, where he teaches at
Emory University, edits Coconut Poetry, and curates the
"What's New in Poetry" reading series. This is his fourth
collection of poetry and his second (*Elapsing Speedway
Organism*, 2006) from No Tell Books.

Also by No Tell Books

2011

Crushes, by Lea Graham

2010

God Damsel, by Reb Livingston

2009

PERSONATIONSKIN, by Karl Parker

2008

Cadaver Dogs, by Rebecca Loudon

2007

The Bedside Guide to No Tell Motel - 2nd Floor, editors
        Reb Livingston & Molly Arden
Harlot, by Jill Alexander Essbaum
Never Cry Woof, by Shafer Hall
Shy Green Fields, by Hugh Behm-Steinberg
The Myth of the Simple Machines, by Laurel Snyder

2006

The Bedside Guide to No Tell Motel, editors Reb Livingston
        & Molly Arden
Elapsing Speedway Organism, by Bruce Covey
The Attention Lesson, by PF Potvin
Navigate, Amelia Earhart's Letters Home, by Rebecca Loudon
Wanton Textiles, by Reb Livingston & Ravi Shankar

notellbooks.org